T0208730

Surviving the Dips of My Unexpected Journey

My Unexpected Journey

Sunshine MaRee

WESTBOW
P R E S S®
A DIVISION OF THOMAS NELSON
& ZONDERVAN

Scripture quotations marked NIV are taken from The Holy Bible, New
International Version®, NIV® Copyright © 1973, 1978, 1984, 2011 by
Biblica, Inc.® Used by permission. All rights reserved worldwide.

Scripture quotations marked NKJV are taken from the New King James Version®.
Copyright © 1982 by Thomas Nelson. Used by permission. All rights reserved.

Scripture quotations marked CSB have been taken from the Christian Standard Bible®,
Copyright © 2017 by Holman Bible Publishers. Used by permission. Christian Standard
Bible® and CSB® are federally registered trademarks of Holman Bible Publishers.

WestBow Press books may be ordered through booksellers or by contacting:

WestBow Press
A Division of Thomas Nelson & Zondervan
1663 Liberty Drive
Bloomington, IN 47403
www.westbowpress.com
1 (866) 928-1240

Because of the dynamic nature of the Internet, any web addresses or links contained in
this book may have changed since publication and may no longer be valid. The views
expressed in this work are solely those of the author and do not necessarily reflect the
views of the publisher, and the publisher hereby disclaims any responsibility for them.

Any people depicted in stock imagery provided by Getty Images are models,
and such images are being used for illustrative purposes only.
Certain stock imagery © Getty Images.

ISBN: 978-1-9736-5447-6 (sc)
ISBN: 978-1-9736-5449-0 (hc)
ISBN: 978-1-9736-5448-3 (e)

Library of Congress Control Number: 2019902042

Print information available on the last page.

WestBow Press rev. date: 02/22/2019

Dedication

To my Daddy and Momma who gave me the strength to carry on. Through my rebelliousness, never did they judge me but always longingly and with care, were standing by my side. They both gave me strength to hold on to my faith; through my journey in life and through this journey of my illness.

Watching their strength, seeing them fight through loss and illness, I could not have been blessed with more Christian, loving parents in this world. I thank God for giving me two flowers from His garden.

With love, remembering them forever and always, for life.

Thank you, Daddy and Momma, your legacy of strength and faith lives on.

Sunshine MaRee

Introduction

Life is a journey, everyone knows that, and everyone has a story. The fact that you are reading this book says that you are interested in knowing mine. I have had many dips along this journey, many struggles, some that I chose for myself and others that came into my life unexpectedly.

Regardless of the dips in the road God never left me, even though I left Him in so many seasons of my life. For so long I made the choice to live behind a mask to veil the confusion and deceit of my life. Although people could see the outcomes of my actions, no one could see the scars or understand the pain that I lived with daily behind the mask that I wore.

Through faith and believing in God the Father and Jesus Christ His Son, I was able to remove the mask, come out of hiding and share with the world what walking my journey of life was and more importantly, what it has become. It is now a walk of faith, with God on my side.

I am completely transparent in this book. There is no more shame in sharing my journey. As difficult as it all was, the Lord has turned my defeats, my pain and my struggles into victory!!

Contents

I   Top of The Hill 1

II   Down the Slope 7

III   Mid-Slide Down the Slope 11

IV   Nearing the Bottom 15

V   Bottom of the Hill 21

VI   The Floor of the Valley 27

VII   Arid Space 33

VIII   Dry Bones 37

IX   Dust of the Bones 45

X   Shadows on the Valley Floor 49

XI   Cresting the Next Hill 53

XII   Sliding Down the Other Side 57

XIII   Sliding Turns to Rolling to the Bottom 65

XIV   Crumpled at the Bottom of the Hill 75

XV   Up the Next Hill 79

XVI   Nearing the top of the Hill 83

XVII   Back on Top of the Hill 87

XVIII Winding Roads 91

My Scriptures of Faith that Brought Me Through!

- Hebrews 13:8 (NIV) "Jesus Christ is the same yesterday and today and forever."

- Psalms 91:16 (NIV) "With long life I will satisfy him and show him my salvation."

- Hebrews 11:1 (NIV) "Now faith is confidence in what we hope for and assurance about what we do not see."

- Proverbs 15:29 (NIV) "The Lord is far from the wicked, but he hears the prayer of the righteous."

- Isaiah 54:17 (NIV) "...no weapon forged against you will prevail, and you will refute every tongue that accuses you. This is the heritage of the servants of the Lord, and this is their vindication from me, declares the Lord."

- Proverbs 11:30 (NIV) "The fruit of the righteous is a tree of life, and the one who is wise saves lives."

- 1 Peter 2:24 (NIV) "He himself bore our sins in his body on the cross, so that we might die to sins and live for righteousness; by his wounds you have been healed."

- Hebrews 12:2 (NIV) "...fixing our eyes on Jesus, the pioneer and perfecter of faith. For the joy set before him he endured the cross, scorning its shame, and sat down at the right hand of the throne of God."

- Psalms 107:1 (NIV) "Give thanks to the Lord, for he is good his love endures forever."

I

Top of The Hill

I was born into a middle-class home, with parents who were Christian, hard working professionals. They were giving, loving, affectionate and very understanding. I was no stranger to hugs and kisses, support and praise. They provided us with everything a child could ever want and dream of. We weren't spoiled by any stretch of the imagination; however, I cannot remember wanting for anything. We were able to travel, visit family in other states and went on family vacations to the beach, things that I now realize were not always the norm for other families that looked like ours during that time. When I watched television shows like 'Leave it to Beaver' I really saw no difference between their family dynamic displayed across the tv screen and mine...they had a short two-story house, the white picket fence and of course the obvious difference of race, but that really didn't register for me at the time.

My parents were providers and protectors, not only physically and materially but also spiritually. I was raised in the Baptist church and was introduced to Jesus at an early age. Both of my parents were very active in church, so of course I was an active participant as well. I attended Sunday school, sang in the youth choir and in the summer attended vacation Bible school. I participated in just about every event hosted by the church. I was baptized at an early age and I did so not only by expectation but also by choice. Dressed in a white robe I was led down a few steps into the baptismal pool. The sounds of the congregation singing a hymn echoed throughout the sanctuary, "wade in the water, wade in the water children, wade in the water, God's gonna trouble the water". In all honesty, I cannot recollect the actual the hymn that was being sung but knowing our tradition it was something along those lines. I went down into the water and when I came up, oh when I came up...I was still me? That public declaration of my acceptance of Christ was just that, it was my letting the world know that I was a believer. Although nothing spectacular happened that morning like the heavens opening, or the ground moving, it made a difference. There was no way for me, being so very young, to understand just how much it would mean to me later in life.

I was the third born, the baby of the family, and I was the only girl. There was only a year between each of us and of course I was the bothersome little sister, but they protected me as big brothers often do. I loved to play with my dolls, and I would try to get my brothers to participate in my tea parties or to help me dress up my dolls and comb their hair, but they were more interested in 'boy stuff'. They enjoyed cars, playing cowboys and Indians, and dirt; no shared interest there for me. When my mother's sister passed away, my cousin came to live with us-she became my sister. We became close and did just about everything together. Although our life trials have been different, and we have had our disagreements, God has blessed us to remain close.

Now my brothers had not one, but two bothersome little sisters to deal with and protect. When they got Go-Carts for Christmas, my sister and I rode them! When they dug a huge whole and made it their club house, my sister and I took it over! I grew up during a time when sitting in the house watching television or playing a video game, we didn't have those then, was something that never crossed our minds. Outside was where we wanted to be. There was always something to do – outside. The neighborhood was teaming with kids and most of the time they congregated on our block, in front of our house. We had foot races, bike races, played hide and go seek, jump roped; you name any game from back-in-the-day and I surely played it. Our house sat on a hill, not a big hill, but just enough to make for an exciting game of King of the Mountain. Some days it seemed as if the entire neighborhood would gather in the front yard and charge ahead, just to see who could conquer the hill and de-throne whomever was King at the time. All in all, the four of us had lots of fun growing up.

When I was eleven, our Mother told us that she was going to have a baby. My sister and I were so excited, a baby! We loved playing with dolls, so in our minds we were getting a real, living, breathing baby doll to dress up and play with. Our brothers were not as excited for some reason, I mean we know they didn't like dolls but who could resist being excited about a baby? I suppose in their minds Momma was too old to have a baby, they seemed a bit embarrassed by the fact, but my sister and I didn't care. When this tiny little girl came home, we showered her with all the love we could.

Being the oldest of the girls, I determined that I would become protector over my sisters, especially the youngest one. Our baby sister went everywhere with my sister and I; to the mall, to the store, over our friend's houses, everywhere we went she was in tow. We decided that this was somehow a help for our Mom. However, we were doing plenty that we shouldn't have without her permission and created more angst than assistance I am sure. One of our helpful decisions resulted in my youngest sister having pierced ears by the time she was two. I think our Mom cried that day, although I cannot be sure if it was from disappointment or due to her trying to hold back from killing my sister and I for making this decision. I would offer an apology at this late date for taking away her choice, but she was just so darn cute we had to adorn her.

Hazel Eyes

I accepted Christ when I was seven years old. I was baptized and came up out of the water feeling that I was safe and that no harm or evil could get to me. I was shielded by Jesus!

I never much paid attention to the color of my eyes, they were light brown but so what they were eyes. Apparently, light eyes had a different effect on teenage boys. It made them creative and imaginative in the "games" that they played, well at least in the games that they played with me. here, the final rule of the game… you had better not tell! I was scared, scared to death of going down to the basement.

As I grew, that fear that I felt in the basement began to permeate my dreams. I would have nightmares of going on vacation with my family and then someone always trying to separate me from them and take me away. It was a recurring dream that visited me each time I closed my eyes. I was so afraid that I would never sleep alone in my room.

One night, a person appeared next to my bedside. The voice was gruff, ugly. It had on red and carried a pitch fork. There were horns on his head and his face was black. He reached out and began to grab hold of me, pulling me from the bed into the darkness. The fear was gripping, but I was able to force out a scream loud enough to wake my parents and my sister who was sleeping in the bed next to mine.

I prayed and cried and rebuked the devil. I prayed, Lord God please do not let him take my life! I had been baptized, come up from the water feeling safe and that nothing could harm me. Apparently, Hazel eyes have an effect on the devil as well.

II

Down the Slope

My interest in boys was slower than most girls my age. I guess I would have been considered a late bloomer. With two brothers in the house I was fully aware of what boys were about. They were messy and loud, and they liked basements. They dug holes in the backyard and made club houses and wouldn't allow girls to come in. They rode go-carts and played basketball and got dirty, sweaty and whew could they smell bad!

No, boys were not really an area of focus for me in elementary school, nor in Junior High. My interests were sewing and cheerleading. I was quite the seamstress and was the first to complete my junior high sewing project. It was a cute little pantsuit with a loud print and bell bottoms. As I stored it away in my cubby for the weekend I was proud, very proud of my creation and my accomplishment. It wasn't a Vera Wang by any stretch of the imagination, but I had put my heart and soul into it; it was a nice pantsuit. When I returned to school the following Monday I found that someone had destroyed it. It was cut into shreds and thrown on the floor. You can imagine my disappointment and hurt, who would do something like this and why do this to me? I never did find out who the culprit was.

I didn't fare much better with cheerleading. I felt great about my try-out, but later was told that I didn't make the squad due to the fact that I didn't like boys. This was certainly a fact that was left off the information regarding try-outs. Had I known this to be the case I am pretty sure I could have pretended. I could have turned my Hazel eyes on some random pre-pubescent dude and made googly eyes at him and sparked his interests. We could have held hands as we walked down the halls to class, with expressionless, blank, forward stares. I could have done this if only I had known. Now, I know, and you know that this was not the reason I didn't make the squad. In truth, this lie was probably concocted by the same girl or girls that destroyed my pantsuit!

After the failed try-out and the pantsuit plunder my focus became school, more explicitly, getting out of this school. My attitude changed. I became angry and agitated each time I stepped off the school bus and those feelings intensified throughout the day. I was surrounded by people, girls who I did not trust, who I did not like and from their words and deeds did not like me. My anger and irritation showed up as fights; in the classroom, in the hallways, when I got on the bus, when I got off the bus. I started skipping class on occasion because I absolutely hated being there. Now days everyone gets involved when children are being bullied. Counselors get involved to try and understand why the child is so upset, and why they are acting out. There was no why that came for me, so I just fought it out. It could have been because I was small in stature and that I didn't weigh much. Or it could have been because I am fair skinned, maybe it was my Hazel eyes, who knows. All I know is that I was a target, but I was the target that fought back. As they say now, I had hands and I was always ready to use them; I was not an easy win by any stretch of the imagination. I couldn't wait to get out and move on to High School where the girls were not as mean and jealous. Surely, they were not so insecure as to be threatened by a pair of pants.

III

Mid-Slide Down the Slope

Remember that I shared that I was baptized? Well I was and yes, I knew the Lord. I was a regular church goer; twice on Sunday, bible study on Wednesday and of course any function held at the church or associated with the church like the National Baptist conventions. We stayed busy and occupied in church. I remember times at church dancing in white robes to the song, Give Me A Clean Heart... give me a clean heart, Lord and I'll follow thee...songwriter Margaret Douroux. As part of the youth choir I learned and listened to the words of the songs we sang. Even those times that I really didn't' want to sing or be in attendance, somehow my favorite song would be on the program. My cousin would stand up and, in his tenor, voice begin to sing, the blood that Jesus shed for me, way back on Calvary, the blood that gives me strength from day to day, it will never lose its power. Songwriter Andre Crouch. This remains one of my favorite songs and an integral part of my testimony.

Now somewhere between the transitions from junior high to high school, fighting and skipping school; not being interested in boys and of course singing in the choir I started trying new things. I figured that I was on the right track in life, even though

I was fifteen, starting high school and still minimally interested in boys, branching out was the thing to do, I mean what could possibly go wrong? Whew, was I naïve—about a whole LOT of things!

Having brothers, I was always around them, boys I mean, but they just didn't peak my interest in the way they did the other girls. Both my brothers were athletes and their friends were always around. These were the jocks and cool guys, the ones that all the girls were trying to get to pay attention to them. It never really made a difference to me, they were just friends of my brothers who hung out at the house from time to time. I would see them sitting in the family room or hanging outside in the drive. I would speak and go on attending to whatever business I had at the time. Every so often one would have something slick to say and I would look, roll my eyes, or say something back and keep it moving. I suppose my proximity to all the desirables, from a high-school girl prospective didn't go over well with the high-school girls. They determined that I was the recipient of the attentions of all the athletes and they didn't like that, and they didn't like me. Had they been smart they would have befriended me, but that was not the case.

I finally decided to try dating, one of those new things I did to branch out. I dated a couple of guys, more so just to have something to talk about with the high-school girls and possibly make them see that I was just me, no threat to them or their love lives. It was never anything serious with a guy, if we broke up, which is what usually happened after a couple of weeks, my world kept revolving and no tears were shed. There were no love notes or poems written in a little diary reflecting on a lost love. I ate ice cream because I like ice cream, not to sooth me and make me feel better because of the breakup. I didn't get angry, I didn't cry, I just kept it moving.

With this whole branching out and dating thing, I learned the meaning of 'party' and went to as many as I possibly could, with or without a date. While education and study should have been the only thing on my mind, my mother was an educator for goodness sakes. I should have been looking forward to graduation and college, planning a future or at least trying to figure out what it was that I wanted in life. Instead, these parties and all the extras that came with them were pushed to the forefront of my thoughts. We partied at the YMCA, we partied at Pizza Hut, we partied at the skating ring, we partied at the basketball games, and the football games; we even partied at the car wash!

One night I stayed out so late that I missed my curfew. I will never forget that night, it was raining, cold and extremely dark. I didn't have a ride, so I started walking. The trek was going to take me hours to make it home and there was no one that I could call for a ride. I knew I was going to be in trouble when I made it home, so I made a decision that seemed plausible, just don't go home! So, I opted to spend the night at a friend's house who happened to live not too far from where I was. She was a bit older than I was, old enough to live on her own and pay rent for the home she lived in. I was banking on her seeing me out in the cold, dark, night air, soaking wet and taking pity on me and allowing me to stay.

It was late, close to 1:00 am when I arrived on her porch and rang the bell. She was awake, although in her pajamas and extremely surprised that I was at the door. She graciously allowed me to come in and agreed to let me stay the balance of the night. I didn't ask to use the phone to call home and tell my parents where I was. No, this night, this very night was the night that I determined that I was grown, and I wasn't going to call. Besides, my Mom and Dad were sleeping soundly, and they needed their rest. I do not know why I made this choice, but I do remember asking myself why I was being so rebellious…" give me a clean heart, Lord and I'll follow thee", songwriter Margaret Douroux, but the thought didn't linger long enough to cause me to make a different choice. I never once took into consideration the worry and fear I caused my parents with that decision. Thankfully, my friend did show concern and called my parents to tell them where I was and that I was alright. Needless to say, when the doorbell rang about 5 minutes later I wasn't surprised.

IV

Nearing the Bottom

The parties were the big topic at school and to be cool you had to be a part of the scene. I wanted to be cool and part of the scene. To better fit in I started smoking cigarettes. KOOL was the popular brand at the time and they were so strong that when I inhaled my head would spin. After some time, I got used to the way that they made me feel so when I started smoking weed the feeling was intensified and I enjoyed it. I perfected my rolling skills quickly. I learned how to separate the seeds and stems, spread a nice even line of leaves down the folded rolling paper, roll it quickly and ever so gently between my thumb and index finger, lick the edge to ensure a secure seal, twist the ends and voila, the perfect joint.

There are two thoughts regarding Marijuana. One side believes that it is non-addictive and that it is not harmful for use while the other side sees it as a gateway drug that leads to the use of harder, more addictive drugs and using alcohol. I suppose I fell somewhere in the middle because I started drinking not long after I began smoking weed. I enjoyed the feeling and began seeking ways to get even higher. The Bible provides us with warnings about the company that we keep. 1 Corinthians

15:33 NIV makes it plain as to what happens to your character based on who you surround yourself with. I can tell you with assurance that this scripture is true. It starts off as curiosity, then develops into a need and before long you are fully engaged. I was so focused on being cool and grown, not much else mattered. You observe others ability to laugh, have fun, joke, or escape the realities of their present situation and you find yourself feeling left out, unable to relate to or tap into the amazing experiences the they were having.

Motivated by the desire to fit in, to please and become a part of it all, I began taking pills. I was finally a part of the cool group and without realizing it, I was becoming even more ostracized from the world.

By this time, I had matured, developed and embraced the fact that these Hazel eyes of mine were one of my best assets. My sister and I were in high school now, and we needed to get around and do our thing. With two hundred dollars saved between the two of us, she and I purchased our first car, a bright yellow VW Bug. Now, neither of us knew how to drive a stick but it didn't matter. We had two brothers and a father that would teach us. Even if they opted not to, we figured it couldn't be that difficult to learn, shoot, we had been stealing our Mom's car for a while now, so we had plenty of practice. Back then you could get your driver's license at 14, so both of us could drive legally and we took every opportunity to do so, unbeknownst to our parents, of course. If we came home and our mother's car was in the drive we considered it an invitation to take it for a quick trip to the Quick Trip around the corner, or to a clothing store and when they opened the new mall, oh boy!

I remember vividly this one time that Mom had left her white station wagon with the wood paneled doors, sitting in the driveway. OK, I know it wasn't the sharpest car around, but it was a car! We found the keys and off we went to the mall. About three quarters of the way there, the car began to overheat so we pulled over to the side of the road, lifted the hood and waited for it to cool off. Smoke was billowing everywhere. We knew a little bit about cars, so we started looking in the back to see if there was antifreeze or something that we could put in the radiator to cool it down. There just happened to be one of those gallon jugs of antifreeze in there and we were elated because we were back in business. Now, I am not sure when it was that we realized it, somewhere between digging through the back of the car and trying to remove the radiator cap without getting sprayed with hot steam, but we looked up and saw that we were stopped right in front of the school where Mom worked!

With a quickness we hurried to get that green glob into that little opening at the top of the radiator. It became a bit awkward trying to accomplish this while keeping our bodies turned and faces out of plain sight so as not to be easily recognizable. I just remember praying that our Mother would not look out the window and discover her two daughters under the hood of her car. Our mall excursion on that day was cut short as we quickly and slowly, yes, quick and slow, drove the car home. We carefully parked it in the drive making sure it was in the same spot that she had left it. We ran inside, placed the keys back where they were and hid in our room for her to come home. When she and Dad came in, they found my sister and I laying across our beds, listening to something on the radio and engrossed in our homework. Neither one of them mentioned anything about the car. When they left the room, we let out a sigh of relief and decided that we were going to have to find an alternate route to the mall. It was many, many years later, we were grown with our own families, before we ever shared that story with our Mom. She was shocked, and I think a bit angry that her girls would do something like that. We left it there and decided to spare her from additional confessions associated with car theft.

We were invincible, or so we thought. My sister and I both worked at the mall and prided ourselves in the clothes, shoes and purses that we wore or carried. If a new style of jean came on the market, we had them before everyone else. Jeans with window pane stitching, jeans with a zipper that ran from the front to the back, yep, we had them first. Leather jackets and purses, the newest fad in tops or pants and of course platform shoes. We would show up at school and everyone was interested in where we got those jeans, where we found that purse and look at those shoes. It didn't hurt that both of us were built either; flat stomachs, nice legs and long hair that we picked out into huge afros. I had a car, I dressed well, I had a nice body and, I had Hazel Eyes.

Then it happened. I met a boy, the boy that would define what I thought love and relationships with the opposite sex looked like. He was tall, handsome, smart and most importantly he was cool. As a matter of fact, he was high ranking cool. He was a year older than I was, but he was mature beyond his age. He had what they call, street cred and everyone knew it. It was not lost on me that I had ascended to a new level of cool as well because I was his girlfriend, his woman and he made sure that everyone knew it. No one bothered me, or he would make sure that they experienced his wrath. I felt safe, protected and a bit like a Queen sitting on the throne. I made sure that everyone knew that I was his lady as well and defended his honor vehemently. I loved this man with everything in me, he became my world.

V

Bottom of the Hill

Being the Lady of the coolest dude around had its perks, but it came with strings attached. For anyone who envied my status, they might have been shocked to know that I was being abused mentally, verbally and physically on a continuous basis. Once, he pushed me from a moving car for no other reason than his anger at something I said or had done, or, simply because he could. He knew he could because I now belonged to him and the child that I was carrying was his as well. Yes, I was now 18 and pregnant, a fact that I had successfully hidden from everyone. I did find solace in the fact that even with all the nonsense I did, skipping school, partying, drugs and running behind the man I loved, I did at least finish high school.

Teen dating violence is much more common place than I believe our society would like to admit. It makes sense however because you have two young people full of hormones and emotions that they are not prepared to manage. I certainly did not have the tools, or the wherewithal to handle the relationship that I found myself in. I was hoping that he would change, and that the abuse would stop but it continued. It didn't matter that I was one hundred pounds lighter and at least a foot shorter than he was. It didn't matter that I was expecting, carrying his offspring, his seed. What mattered to him was the drugs, the money and of course the street cred; what would he look like if he couldn't keep his woman in check. What mattered more than anything were these three things; my obedience, my loyalty and that I could take a punch.

I worked throughout my pregnancy. Every day I got up, cleaned up, hid my bruises and headed out the door to my job. One bright, clear September morning, I was sitting in stalled traffic on the overpass of the interstate. It was about 9:00am, the sky was clear and bright, the sun was warm, and I was bopping to something playing on the radio of my new 1978 Camaro. It was shaping up to be a good day, and regardless of the delay I was enjoying myself on this morning. Suddenly, I felt a terrible jolt from behind. The force of the impact sent my brand new 1978 Camaro half way over the guard rail of the highway. It happened so quickly that it took a bit of time for my mind to register what was going on. When I tried to move I realized that my baby bump of six and a half months was wedged through the hole in the steering wheel. My car, with me in it, was hanging over the guard rail of the over pass, one move too quickly or in the wrong direction could send this car plummeting to the highway below. I hung there suspended over the rail, scared, unable to move. The fear was overwhelming, matched only by the pain in my stomach which had begun almost immediately after the crash.

I knew of only one thing to do and so I did it, I cried out to the Lord. "Jesus, please send someone to help me". My eyes were full of tears, my body wracked with pain and my heart was full of fear. I didn't know if the car was going over the rail, if I was going to be able to walk, but more than anything I feared for the life of my unborn child. There was a couple who saw what had happened and came to the car to help. Of course, there was nothing they could do for me, but their presence was a welcomed comfort.

Traffic had begun to move, and I could hear the horns blaring as they went around. I laid my head on the steering wheel, crying and praying. Through my tears I saw a big Red Ball delivery truck pull up next to me. The driver didn't get out of the cab, instead he just lingered long enough to peer inside of the car, nosey. It wasn't until he sped away that my brain connected to the reality that he was the culprit; he was the person who had rear-ended me and placed me in this life-threatening predicament. Thankfully the couple with me had seen the entire thing and was able to give the information to the authorities when they arrived on the scene. The ambulance finally arrived, and they got me out of the car, onto a gurney and as they loaded me into the ambulance I mouthed the words, thank you to the couple God sent to me that fateful September morning.

As they wheeled me through the emergency room I saw a man there asking the nurses had anyone been brought in from a wreck earlier. He seemed frazzled, anxious and distracted, so much so that he didn't pay attention that it was me on the stretcher when they ran past him to the emergency room. I cringed when I realized it was him, how could he have left me there and why was he here at the hospital? Was it not enough to leave me hanging over the railing of that interstate and show no concern for my wellbeing? For all I knew he might have been there to finish the job, or at least that is what my mind considered. I was scared. The gurney burst through the double doors that lead to the ER beds at a feverish pace. They rounded a corner and as they neared the bed they were going to transfer me to I saw another familiar face, but this one brought me a sense of peace. It was my Daddy. I have no idea how he made it to the hospital before I did, but he was a fireman, so maybe it came across their radio and he recognized the description of the car and the driver. When I think about it now, that would have taken him a bit longer to get the notification. I have no way of verifying this, however I suspect that it wasn't his station that got the message to him. Instead it was his CB friends who keyed their mics and broadcast the information, and Cougar hit the cement slab: 10-4 and we rollin.

It didn't matter to me how he got there, I just remember that he spoke two simple words and I felt a wave of peace wash over me, "I'm here."

It's funny the things that are said when no one thinks you are listening. As the doctor's pushed medication into me to try and stop the labor and ease my pain I heard the contradictory conversations; 'this is not good', 'you are doing fine'. As my condition continued to worsen, I heard the doctor's say, 'it is going to be her or the baby'. I remember thinking, no, no, no, this can't be. This can't be the only choice; so, I quickly prayed, "Lord, please save us both". I prayed, and I prayed... and prayed. Finally, after pumping me with medication after medication to no avail, the doctors decided they could not stop my labor, the baby was coming. It took some time but that following day my son was born. He weighed in at four pounds and was about the size of the palm of my hand. His lungs were under developed but he was alive and so was I. God had answered my prayers, HE spared both of our lives.

The drugs used to hold off my labor were so strong that my legs were affected and of no use for the time being. I had to learn how to walk again, but that didn't matter to me. My baby boy was alive! They would wheel me down to the NICU at the hospital and I would sit next to him in the incubator and just wonder at the fact that he was even here. He was so tiny and fragile laying there. He had tubes everywhere; in his nose, a tube in his mouth, IV's in his little arms. He was so small, I was amazed that the needles didn't go all the way through him.

With babies born this early and with this much trauma things can turn for the worse in seconds. I made it a point to be in the room with him every moment that I could. I continued in therapy and it wasn't long before I was walking down to the NICU to spend the days with my son. When it came time for me to be discharged, it was extremely difficult to leave that hospital without him, but time was needed for his lungs to develop and for him to put on weight. I was overjoyed when I was able to bring him home for the first time. I remember thinking, here I am a teenager, unmarried and now I have a baby. I was at a loss as to what was going on with my life at this point, I did know that the Lord had kept us; HE saved us and spared us for a reason.

VI

The Floor of the Valley

Although I was in a relationship, it was as though I was a single parent because all of the responsibility of raising my children fell on me. Sadly, we were not the priority. I cannot explain the "why?" behind my taking him back time and time again, but I did. The best I can come up with, is simply that, I had been conditioned to be obedient and loyal. In those times when I forgot my "role as a wife", I was quickly reminded with a slap, a kick or a punch to the face.

While the physical abuse was painful, I endured it, remember, I could take a punch; it was the mental and emotional abuse that would land the most detrimental of blows. Those were the slow healing scars, the ones that became infected. I was convinced that I was in love and love endures all things, bears all things and love never fails. Love is also blinding, and I could not see my way out, so I stayed. Before long, my life turned into a whirlwind and began to spiral out of control. I had become septic from life and too weak to walk away from it all. The constant fighting and continuous abuse would not let up, so I began to self-soothe and turned to drugs. They were always available thanks to my the love of my life, and I could indulge as much as I wanted, or so I thought. What I had chosen, as my way of escape quickly turned into a steel, cold, gray vault with the door closing slowly behind me. It is amazing how confused a person can become with the situations in life. I could feel the world, my life closing in on me, that light shining through that vault surrounding was narrowing. Oh, wait, let me smoke this and then snort a little of that and I would be fine. Yes, the drugs provided the illusion that the vault door was still standing open.

I had so many things happening in my life at the time it was impossible to determine which way was right and which way was wrong. My drug habit became expensive, and my bank account was empty. My unlimited access became limited, so I turned to the streets to ensure I had money to take care of a few things; one, pay my bills and keep a roof over our heads. Two, clothes on my child's back and three, my drug habit. I was sitting on the sidelines of my life watching it ebb slowly away into the darkness. From time to time I would find a bit of strength and in those moments, I would begin to question myself. I was not raised like this, where were my senses? I knew better, I deserved better, I am better. However, I didn't want help and no, I didn't want to stop, no! I amazed myself at how weak I had become. I was fully convinced that there was no way out of this life. So, I changed the way I dressed so that I could hide the scars on my body. I put on a mask to hide the scars from the damage of the drugs and from the streets. I hid behind the mask, so no one could see.

Addiction was a gradual process for me, it did not happen immediately. I was still able to function; I took care of the house, my child and was able to stay employed. My appearance did not change, I had always been petite so no changes there. I had always keep myself groomed and dressed well; no changes there. Oh, and my hazel eyes were still just as beautiful and alluring as they had ever been. If you engaged me in conversation I was clear, and concise, although my position on certain topics could be considered questionable. To be honest, if you did not have a view behind the veil that I had created, anyone who did not know me personally had no idea of the darkness that I was struggling with.

It did not take long before the darkness encompassed me; it demanded satisfaction. I had an addition that needed to be managed, however I had limited resources to make that happen. I had to be creative in funding my addiction and before long I realized that I had access to resources, right at my fingertips, that I could utilize to fulfill my desires. At the time I had an excellent job where I was trusted to handle money that was coming into the company. I do not believe it necessary for me to list all the gory details, so I will sum it up in one word-forgery. You see I believed that the veil that I created to surround my darkness was also a protective barrier and made me invincible, invisible and impervious to being caught. I was wrong. When I was arrested I was confident that I would not see the inside of a jail cell because I had support, people who were there with me in the darkness behind the veil. I had been good to them, supportive of them; I was not a selfish addict, no I was not. When I serviced my addiction, I also made sure everyone else was serviced as well. I was going to be just fine.

Here is something that I will share with you, a word of advice regarding the people that you surround yourself with; they will always do what it is to preserve and protect themselves, even if it means sacrificing you! Everyone who I thought would protect me did not. Those who knew what lied behind the veil and enjoyed the benefits of it were the very people who sang like a Mockingbird when confronted by the law. By the time the story was complete you would have thought me some crafty financial mastermind, which of course was not the case. I was an addict who exercised an opportunity and now I was going to jail to pay for my crimes. I could have easily spilled the tea and took down several others, but I didn't. I held my tongue.

The sound of metal against metal as the bars to my cell were closed sent a feeling like no other though my being. That vault door was finally closed, not even a sliver of light creeped in. I came to the realization that I had trusted man to protect me and made him my choice instead of God. I opted to believe that a man would somehow place my best interests above his own and come to my rescue, even with plenty of evidence, a lifetime of evidence, to support the contrary.

I felt broken, alone, abandoned and betrayed. The emotions swirled around inside of me with the velocity of a catastrophic tornado and tore the veil that I had so skillfully created into shreds and laid it around my feet in a heap. I hurt. My cries came from deep within my soul. Everything inside wretched and twisted and spewed from me as a guttural weep. It was days before I could stop crying but when I did I saw that my tears had washed away the remnants of that veil.

My eyes were red and swollen from all the crying, but my vision was clearer than ever before. There was no desire to excuse away the many wrong choices that I had made in my life; not just the current situation but all of them. No one outside of myself was responsible, there was only me and at that moment I chose to admit and own it all. My next move, and without hesitation, was the lifting of head. Then, I lifted my hands. Just a I had taken ownership of all the mess in my life, I gave it all away; I gave it to God. I asked for forgiveness and, I prayed for increased faith so that I could trust HIM at his word. I thanked HIM for my life, I thanked him for JESUS my Savior who pinned all the nonsense that had been my life to the cross so that I could make a different choice. With my choice I was reconnected to my source; I am now a new creature, a new person. The Spirit of the Living God is now alive, well and working inside of me. I recognize now that all the storms and doubts, mistakes and challenges that I made brought me to this place of grace. HE knows all that I was to become and what it was going to take to get me through the challenges that I faced.

I did my time and it wasn't easy. I found out that my Hazel eyes have a similar effect on women who have been incarcerated for a while. This meant I had to protect myself, through time I garner some respect and the overt advances stopped. When my release date came I left that place without one friend, and the satisfaction of knowing that no one ever took me down. This gave me a sense of accomplishment and the idea that I could handle anything.

With this new-found freedom came confidence. I was stronger now and sure of the path that I was taking. This confidence led me back home and back into the arms of the man I loved. In my mind I was sure that things would be different because I was different. The drugs were out of my system, and my head was clear. A couple of years later I found out that I was pregnant, again. I wasn't ready. I wasn't prepared to do this alone, not with two children and not with him. So, I made the decision to get away, to leave him. If I had to do this by myself then I would do so, by myself. I moved out of state. My daughter was born, and I was on my way to a new life. I had moved to a big city full of life and opportunity. I was on my way. I was free. I was the mother of two amazing children, I had overcome! It took about two months for my victory to wear thin.

VII

Arid Space

I am reminded of the scripture in Matthew12:43-45:(NIV) "When an impure spirit comes out of a person, it goes through arid places seeking rest and does not find it. Then it says, 'I will return to the house I left.' When it arrives, it finds the house unoccupied, swept clean and put in order. Then it goes and takes with it seven other spirits more wicked than itself, and they go in and live there. And the final condition of that person is worse than the first.

There was never a truer depiction of this scripture than what became of my life as I went willingly back to the lies, the cheating, the drugs and the abuse, only this time it was much worse.

I remember one snowy winter night that I thought I would die. It was like a drummer beating his drum on a cold weather night. Every stroke felt like the pulsating sound of a drum... boom boom boom...I felt every beat. I heard the sound if my children screaming. It's like I wasn't there just numbed from the blows. Then I felt a warmth running down my face. I realized that I couldn't hear anymore. I could only feel a drip, drip.

Finally, it was over, or so I thought. I looked in the mirror and saw ear that my ear was hanging on by a thread! There was blood all over the table. The hospital wasn't far from where we lived, but I didn't have a car. It was windy and cold and impossible to think that I could manage the six-block walk to the hospital with my children. It would have taken at least two additional hands to manage an infant baby in my arms while clasping my torn and bloody ear and holding on to my then six-year-old. I had no choice but to leave my children and head for the hospital. I had all kinds of emotions. I was angry, but the anger wasn't directed at my children. As I looked around trying to figure out what to do, I saw my love looking satisfied with what was done, the near detachment of my ear. Time was of the essence and I knew I needed to get to the hospital. I felt comfortable that they would be alright staying put. Hours later I returned home with the 25 stiches it took to re-attach my ear, and the bonus of finding out that I had been given a STD, only to find that my children had been left home alone.

My life had become a twisted game of hide and seek. My children and I running and hiding in all sorts of places, basements and shelters. Running and hiding from drug dealers who spoke no English. I would do what I could to be safe, and when things calmed down I would go back. I would move into a wonderful place and stay for a time and then have to move out because that was just the way my life worked. I found myself seeking my belongings regularly. I would come home and find everything gone. Everything from televisions to small appliances and entire houses full of furniture. Those times when I had a car were especially fun, I'll call this game, find the Ford. This is how you play. I go to work and while I am at work, someone comes and takes my car. I get off from work, find that my car is gone, and I call the police. The police take the information and use it to locate my vehicle-game over. More often than not, it was usually found in the possession of someone who dealt drugs, probably as collateral for payment, or in lieu of payment. Sadly, it happened so much that some of the operators at AAA would recognize my voice when I called and would address me by name!

It never mattered where I moved or where I went, I would always be found. It never mattered what locks and alarms I placed on the doors, I still was not safe. When a person is relentless, there is not lock that is going to stop them, there is no window or door that is going to keep them out. Whenever I refused to give in to the demands, the violence began again. It became a strong, emotionally manipulative and violent type of relationship.

I was thrown down a flight of concrete stairs with the same ease as you would toss a tissue into the trash. As I tried to hide the scars and the abuse, it became more and more comfortable with beating me publicly. There was increasingly less and less concern for appearances and more concern for making me pay for my disobedience and disloyalty. I remember riding peaceably in the car and out of nowhere tensions began to rise. It was always about something small or nothing at all, this is how it usually went. There in the middle of a busy intersection the car stopped, I was grabbed by the neck and my head was repeatedly bashed into the steering wheel, the dashboard and then the gear shaft. I cried out to Jesus, "Please help me, I'm going to be killed in front of my children!!". At that moment the door of the car opened, and I told my children to run, call the police and get help.

At home, the simplest of chores could prove to be dangerous. While ironing my clothes one morning we had an exchange of heated words. I guess I had talked too much because the iron was snatched from my hand I was being choked with the cord. My head was placed on the ironing board and then the hot iron was placed to the side of my face! I am of a fair complexion, so the burning was going to be noticeable. If my screams were not enough, I endured the pain of hearing my children screaming outside of the locked door. In that moment I saw my death. Again, I prayed and again the Lord answered. This time it was the sound of the door being kicked open and three angels in blue uniforms coming to my rescue. Domestic abuse laws were not as strict as they are now, so in order to make sure that I could live in peace again I let the officers know about the outstanding warrants. On the way to the hospital to treat the burns, all I could think of was that I wanted to go home to my parents' house, but I couldn't. I could not let them see me like this. Fortunately, I was blessed that the burns were not 3rd degree and my face would heal, but it was going to take some time. So, I did what I did best, I put on quite a bit of foundation to cover up the pattern the iron left on my face and pretended all was well.

VIII

Dry Bones

I wish that I could tell you that things get better from here, but that would not be the truth, it just isn't my truth. There's always the constant reminder and thoughts about living your life around a skilled abuser and that you could receive a blow any place any time. I was brought up to value family and marriage. I really wanted a good marriage. But once again, the cycle continued and this time after incarceration there was a desire to seek vengeance upon me. There were more challenges ahead and I was so used to the abuse. I had become accustomed to my own type of nightmare but admittedly unprepared for what life was going to throw my way next.

The year was 1985 and I was in pain. Excruciating pain radiated all over my entire body. There were days where I could not get out of bed and my headaches were crippling. After a myriad of tests, the doctor returned a diagnosis of Rheumatoid Arthritis. They could not tell me the why behind the diagnosis, but there is a possibility that it is hereditary. They also believe that factors in the environment may also trigger the activation of the immune system for people who may be susceptible. My symptoms were acute. The disease effects the autoimmune system of the body, so my body fights and destroys itself and as a result, my joints swell and my bones degenerate. I lose weight with the medications; I gain weight from the steroids. I have had every treatment there is for this disease to the point that my body cannot tolerate a lot of drugs. I even had gold shots. They were expensive and ineffective as was, and is, everything else that has been used. As I tried to make the adjustments to what my new life would be living with this debilitating disease, I received a call from my brother who lived in Denver. His words were so comforting and supportive.

Comforting, supportive, kind, comical, athletic, fearless, godly and loving. These are only a few of the adjectives that I can associate with my brother. He was tall and handsome and wonderful, and... he died. In the same month that I found out that I had Rheumatoid Arthritis, he was diagnosed with acute Leukemia. He worked for a national delivery service and banged into things regularly, so bruises showing up on his body were not anything to cause pause or alarm. It wasn't until his energy started to drop and the bruises would not heal that the siren went off. When he told me the diagnosis my heart fell to my feet and tears rushed like the rapids down my cheeks. My stomach turned sour in an instant and I had to fight the urge to vomit. I prayed and asked the Lord if there was something, anything that I could do to help him. My world was again torn apart with the news, my brother was in a fight for his life and there was nothing that I could do.

After talking to my brother, I collected myself enough to speak, I wanted to share what the doctors said about me. I thought that maybe this would at least bring some consolation in the house. As expected there was no reaction to the news of my illness. As a matter of fact, I believe there was a sense of satisfaction that now chasing me to land a blow wouldn't exert as much energy because of my condition because I wouldn't have the strength to fight back. I shared the news about my brother as well, but I am not sure whether it was understood clearly what my brother's diagnosis meant. What I do know is that the response absolutely amazed me. Most of the exchange is a blur, but what is very clear in my memory is that sharing the news about my brother resulted in my being thrown down a flight of stairs to the basement and trying to lock me down there. I learned that evening that there is a distinct difference between mean and evil.

That year I traveled back and forth to Denver to visit my brother. There were times when the kids were in school and couldn't come with me, so they stayed home. It scared me to leave them. I kept thinking and hoping that since I made a change in my life, maybe there's still hope for my marriage. Maybe taking on the responsibility for them without me around would spark something inside, some sort of paternal instinct and that would make you want to be and do better for your children, for me, for us. My last visit with my brother before his death I didn't have my children with me. He and I visited for a bit and then he told me to go home. Very pointedly he said, "go home and get your kids, they're not being taken care of". It wasn't what he said, but more in the way that he said it, like he had been a witness to what was going on in my absence. There was such a conflict raging inside of me. I wanted to stay with my brother, but I knew I needed to get to my kids. My internal battle came to an immediate halt with his next words. "Leave, go home. I am alright. I am going home as well; home to be with the Lord. I am alright."

Upon my return I found that the responsibility of taking care of my children had been handed to someone else. I was so disappointed as I had hoped and prayed that my kids would finally see the paternal role model that they needed, but that didn't happen. Well at least he had made one sound decision to take my kids to a safe place. The other decision was not. You see, when I left home I had a house full of furniture, but when I returned my entire house was empty. I was told that someone had broken in and stolen everything. I was upset, not so much because everything was gone but more so that I was at this place yet again. I played the role pretending to believe the story and probably secretly hoping that it was true. As I stood in the front yard looking around, trying to determine which neighbor to interview to see who saw what, the little lady across the street filled me in with all the juicy details. There was no burglary (there went my hopes), it was intentional. It was happening again. She told me that people I knew backed the truck up in my yard and loaded it with all my household wares and drove away.

A week later my brother was gone. He was with Jesus and I was in the car being berated, cursed, belittled and beaten up the highway as we traveled to attend my brother's funeral. That's what you get when you don't believe the lie (about the burglary) and you state the fact that you don't believe it. A lie doesn't care who tells it, but there can be consequences when you expound the truth. It didn't matter much what was going on, or what was being said, I was distracted by the memory of my brother and his final words to me, "I am alright". He had such a calming peace about him and an assurance of where he was going that he was comforting everyone who saw or spoke with him.

My brother was a very special man. He was loved and highly thought of by so many, and it seemed that they all had come to pay their respects. There was a house full of family to visit with so that is what I did. All afternoon and evening I spent time with this person and that person. Cousins and old friends that I had not seen in years. My sister had been watching me throughout the day, and she had noticed that I was distancing myself a lot from him. If he came into a room I left. If I couldn't leave the room I moved as far away as possible. I savored each moment I didn't could be away. At one point in the afternoon my sister pulled me aside and asked what was going on, she knew something was wrong. I wanted to take her to a quiet room, close the door and lay across a bed like we used to and just tell her everything. Instead I promised that we would talk later, and we walked arm in arm to the kitchen to grab something to nibble on. That night, the night before the home going service, I was beaten severely for looking at other men; men who for the most part were family or long-time family friends. As a skilled abuser and the blows were done in places that weren't visible. Again, because of my complexion being so light, any bruising would've been noticeable. I was able to conceal the burses under the dress I wore to the funeral. Trust me, this was not jealousy, nor was it love. There was no concern about me and we both knew it. The return trip home was quiet. The kids were playing in the back seat and the trip for me was quiet. All I heard was my brothers voice in my head, "I'm alright".

After returning home from my brother's funeral, the days and years began to run together, and again nothing changed. Living in shelters while druggies and drug dealers enjoyed the comforts of my apartment. Back and forth between the apartment and shelters with my children. Although some of these places were awful with garbage strewn about and filthy floors, they were a refuge from the misery at home. But at times home had its perks. From time to time and after one of those times I found myself pregnant, again. I never planned any of my pregnancies, but I felt blessed each time I knew that I had a new life and a new love inside of me. As always, I was hopeful that this time, this pregnancy would be the time that would change this cycle. I wanted to be seen as valued, to be truly loved and cared for because I was carrying our child. I am not sure if it was a conscience decision to beat it out of me or if it was an accidental occurrence, but I ended up losing the baby. I found solace in this song lyric that says 'The blood, that gives me strength from day to day, it will never lose its power'...songwriter Andre Crouch

I tried to resign myself to the reality that I had created. I kept trying to accept this was going to be my life; abuse and devastation, sickness and chronic pain. I kept trying to give up and the harder I tried, the more a small, still voice kept saying, 'run to Jesus, He is the only way out'. No, this is my life. I accept it as it is, it will never change. 'Run to Jesus, He is the only way out'. This inward exchange went on for years until that little voice made a statement that changed my mind, 'don't ask God how much it will take to pull you out, but how much will you take before you finally leave?' Just as soon as I gathered up my senses and determined that I was leaving, he did something that surprised me, and it gave me hope, he asked me to officially marry him and I did.

Oh, I'm sorry, I need to clarify things for you. Although I treated my relationship like a marriage, the truth is that we were only legally married for a year. I am sure that you are shaking your head and probably a bit confused as to why someone would endure all of this at the hands of someone who had not even given you his last name? I wish that there was an answer, something that would make sense but there isn't.

After about six months of marriage I noticed a change in my body. An unusual change to my 'Lily'. Oh, no! I went to the doctor to have her checked out, all the while plotting my revenge if I had been given some sort of STD. As I laid on that table I thought of all the things that I could and would do to him if any of these tests came back positive for anything other than a really bad yeast infection. My hospital records documented the years of abuse; I could use the battered woman's syndrome as a defense. 'it's going to take us a couple of days for all of your results to come back, we'll give you a call'. I thought of all types of stuff to get even. If he's high I could bash his head in, push him down some steps and say that he fell. Naw, he may not bounce correctly. Forget it, I would just stab or shoot him and be done with it. Somehow, being legally married to the man gave me a new-found strength to leave him.

It took about a week for my test results to come in. It was 1990 and my life was getting ready to go into a rather a rapid spin. I had been consumed with planning my, soon-to-be ex's demise. While I hate to admit it, I derived immense pleasure in the idea that I would be the one to end his life. I believe the results of those tests saved his life.

IX

Dust of the Bones

I heard Maya Angelou refer to words as things, and I believe that. Cancer is a word. Cancer is a thing. This thing had invaded my body and attached itself to my cervix. All I could think of in that moment was my children, what would happen to them. This was not the way things were supposed to go. I was finally free from the chains of my marriage and now this! My head was spinning, I was confused and feeling defeated. Just as the overwhelming feelings of despair closed in I closed my eyes and prayed the simplest of prayers, "Lord, keep me in your arms. Please heal my body".

My surgery was scheduled quickly. My parents were with me in the room as they prepped me for the procedure. As I laid there, groggy from the medications to calm me I overheard the doctor as he read the results of the additional tests they had run. It was too late; the cancer had already spread to my uterus. I watched the expressions on my parents face as he told them the prognosis. The Oncologist told us that my life would culminate in approximately three months. I searched for words, something that I could say that might comfort them. With tears running down my face I gave them the only truthful words I could think of that would stick, I love you.

The love of God always amazes me. HE is omnipresent and hears us when we make our requests. One simple prayer, prayed. One simple prayer answered. The cancer had not spread as the doctor's initially thought. They had performed a hysterectomy and were confident that they were able to get all the cancer in doing so. One simple answered prayer changed the shipwreck of my life. The Lord healed my body and my life. For the next fifteen years, my life was full and rich. I was single again now that I was divorced. I returned to church and became as active as possible. I had an excellent job at an aircraft plant and I made a very nice salary. It felt wonderful knowing that I made more than enough money to take care of my little family.

I will not pretend that I didn't have struggles because I did. My job in aircraft laid me off not once, but twice, but both times I was called back. My son and daughter were well into their teens and I had to deal with all the teenager things and then some. During this time, I was blessed with my first grandchild, a beautiful baby boy who stole my heart.

I battled RA with all the headaches and joint pain, even still, I was at peace. Finally, my health declined to the point that I could not longer to continue to work. I was in and out of the hospital on a continuous basis. People were always asking me what I was going to do, some out of concern and others out of curiosity, and others just to have something to talk about. I filed for disability to take care of myself and my family, and with my extensive medical history you would think that I would be approved without issue. They denied my claim not once, but twice. I was beginning to get discouraged but I persisted and applied a third time. This time I was approved, thank you, Jesus. It wasn't a lot of money; however, it was enough to allow us to live in a nice apartment complex and to meet the monthly obligations. There was also enough for a few extras, not a lot of non-essentials but some. You see, one small prayer prayed, and one small prayer answered changed my life. I still had struggles and challenges with life and with my health, but I had a peace that went past anything that I understood.

X

Shadows on the Valley Floor

Year after year, I have managed my life with RA. The pain and challenges of your bones deteriorating is uncomfortable to say the least, but I never allowed it to stop me. No, I never allowed sickness to get in my way. One thing that was a constant in my life was that I was continually at one doctor or another. It was 2005, and time to get a physical along with my well woman check and mammogram. Having lived with RA for so long, I simply blamed all my sickness and pain on the disease. When the physician did the breast exam and found a lump in my left breast, and decided that the lump was enough of a concern that it warranted a biopsy I couldn't blame the RA.

In the recesses of my mind the whispers began…" cancer, you have cancer", that 'thing' had returned. I so wanted the results to come back negative, and to have the doctor tell me that it was nothing but that was not the case. The results of the biopsy came back positive. I tried to be attentive and listen as the doctor showed me the films and discussed the treatment options, but, I was stunned, or maybe I was in shock. I heard everything that was being said, and gave nods affirming my understanding, but honestly it was falling on deaf ears. My brain was on overload, I

49

could not think about treatments, or anything else. My mind was overtaken with only one question and internally I kept asking it repeatedly, why God?

After everything that I had overcome, everything that I had endured, everything that HE had brought me through, why was I having to go through this? I listened intently for that still, small voice to respond to my questioning, however it did not come in the form of words, or a vision. Instead, my answer came in the form of a feeling of peace and assurance. So, as the doctor continued to educate me on the mechanics of the procedure I was to undergo, I prayed, thanking the Lord for taking care of me. I knew that whatever the outcome, HE would be with me.

I had a very short time to try and adjust to everything. I went from being dazed and reeling from the news, to being sedated and undergoing Lumpectomy surgery a week later. They put me under a general anesthesia and put me to sleep. When I came to in the recovery room the surgeon was there and told me that they were able to get all of the cancer. They had successfully removed the cancerous lump, and no lymph nodes were involved. The surgeon told me that he had also removed enough of the surrounding tissue that could possibly contain additional cancerous cells that he did not feel that radiation was needed. I am not sure what the differences were in my case, however this was one of the worst procedures I have ever had. My doctor came to check on me after the procedure and after a quick check he assured me that I was going to be just fine. He told me that I was lucky. I quickly corrected him, I am blessed.

After facing down cancer for the second time, I decided that it was time for me to get a new perspective on life, go somewhere else and start fresh. I saw my life as a puzzle where some of the pieces fit and other pieces were forced into place. I could remove take those misfit pieces and turn them around, search and put them in their rightful place, but that seemed like a waste of time. I had grown tired of the same faces and the same places; tired of all the RA doctors telling me there was nothing else that they could do. I had heard that Kansas City had a lot of great RA doctors who had conducted recent studies in RA with some promising results, so that is where I determined I would move. My daughter was apparently feeling the same way, so we packed up and moved.

As we drove onto I-35, I began to reminisce about my life, and the memories came flooding in. Some bad, and some good. Yes, my life was a puzzle, full of worn and crooked pieces, some of the corners turned up, plenty forced into places where they didn't fit; a faded and worn picture, but one thing is sure—I had lived.

XI

Cresting the Next Hill

I was so excited with the prospect of finding a new physician to treat my RA that after getting settled it became my first order of business. I went from one doctor to the next, yep, one after the other just to hear that there was nothing that they could do. My condition was rare and difficult because my system would no longer tolerate the drugs that they had to treat it. At the point where I was about to give up I met a doctor who said with confidence, the he could treat me, and that he could get me to the place of wellness. He discussed his plan for treatment and the drugs he was going to use, oh he was confident and unwavering in his claims, even as I told him that my body would not tolerate some of the medications he included in his treatment plan. Amid my protests, he held my hands and said, "trust me, this will work."

Now, I am not sure which drug it was that caused me to have a stroke, nor which one it was that caused my kidneys to fail, but I am sure of one thing, the treatment didn't work and my trust in this doctor and anything that he said was gone! I am blessed that I did not suffer any impairment from the stroke or the kidney failure. With time my health improved. I was no longer able to take any medications for the RA, but continued with infusions, and managed the pain with prayer and an unwavering faith that I would eventually be healed, all in Gods time.

My Dads health had begun to fail even more, and I was traveling back and forth checking on him and my Mom, doing what I could to assist my sister in their care. They had moved into an assisted living facility, but both were in the beginning stages of dementia and the challenges were increasing. As I watched their health decline, I started thinking that it would probably be a good idea to get some additional life insurance, just to make sure that I could leave something for my children to cover expenses if something happened to me. It was on my mind, however as we often do I had delayed in acting. Then, my aunt passed away and getting additional coverage moved to the forefront of my mind and became a priority.

I had one policy that I have had for years, but I wanted more. I wasn't sure if I would even qualify because of the myriad of health issues, but I decided that it was worth a try. I had renter's insurance through one of the major insurance providers, so I reached out for information and one of their insurance agents contacted me. We conversed for a while and I shared my health history and after hearing myself talk I changed my mind, thanked him and ended the conversation. The man called me repeatedly, even after I told him no, he continued call. He stated that it would only take a couple of questions and a blood test and they could write the policy. If for no other reason than to get him to leave me alone, I set up the appointment, went in for the blood test, answered the questions and waited. I waited. I waited. He was insistent before, almost to the point of harassment and now nothing? I finally decided that they had denied me coverage and he just didn't have the nerved to call me and say so.

It had been a couple of weeks since the passing of my aunt, attending her funeral and not hearing back from the insurance agent. I had pretty much dismissed the idea of adding more insurance and my life was returning to my type of normal. I was on the phone with my youngest sister discussing nothing specific and everything in general when the mail was delivered. I casually reviewed each envelope and tossed it aside; bill, bill, coupon, bill and then I looked at the large, brown envelope from the insurance company. It contained a huge packet of information full of all sorts of documents with a letter on top. I began to read the letter thinking it to be instructions on how to complete the paperwork, but as I read further the words made no sense.

They explained their testing procedures, named the lab that they used, how the samples were treated; then stated that I had tested positive for a liver disease, specifically Hep-C and suggested that I see my regular physician. Wait, what? I read it again, Hep-C? I screamed into the phone and began to cry. I had been reading through the letter with my sister still on the phone; she was at a loss as to what to do. She did her best to calm and comfort me, but it was of no use. I broke down and wept, from the depths of my soul, I wept.

XII

Sliding Down the Other Side

I cannot be sure of what it was that I was expecting when I contacted my RA doctor. I spoke to the nurse and cancelled my infusion and then shared with her the information from the insurance company, however I can assure you that I was not expecting what came next. The nurse stated that she would relay the message to the doctor and abruptly hung up the phone. She called me back within minutes and told me to come in so that they could re-run the tests. I went, completed a battery of tests and was given a new appointment date later in the week to return to discuss my results. It was probably the quickest turn around on labs that I have ever experienced!

When I walked into the office, what once was a bright hello from the receptionist was more of a snarl or maybe it was a low growl. The nurse who usually smiled and asked me how I was doing never opened her mouth. She escorted me to an exam room, opened the door and stood back and waited for me to enter. She pointed to the scale for me to get on it so that she could weigh me, almost ordered me to take a seat and then put the BP cuff around my arm. I am pretty sure she inflated it much more than necessary and ripped it from my arm quite aggressively as it were a failed attempt at choking me to death.

Typically, doctors are held in high regard, even to the point of reverence for those considered the best in their field. We often forget that they are human beings with feelings and failures, just like everyone else. I anticipated that he, my doctor, would be just as moved by this shocking report as I was. When he entered the room, I studied his face, looking for a sympathetic glimmer in his eyes, the corners of his mouth upturned into a gentle smile, a perplexed and furrowed brow. He was of course the one who had told me to 'trust him'.

He offered no greeting, no hand shake, no smile, he offered me nothing. He moved past me in the room, threw the chart on the counter and turned his back to me. Over his shoulder he commented that it was a good idea to try to get extra insurance if I had to live my life in a nursing home. What? When he finally turned to face me, he was scowling and began to defend his practice. He went on and on about how clean his office is, how they sterilize all their equipment, how everyone uses gloves. At this point I must admit that I was a bit confused, why was he saying all of this? He continued his rant until I couldn't take it anymore. His tone had now become aggressive, so I got up, collected myself, and told him that he had no right or reason to talk to me in this manner. As he formed his mouth to say something else, he quickly became acquainted with an older version of me. James 3 gives the best example of how deadly the tongue can be and is. I cursed this man something fierce, however, I do not feel it beneficial to include the words in this book. I will leave them out and allow you to use your creativity in stringing together the most vile, profane words you can imagine.

For all the progress that I thought I had made, it seemed as if I were back at the start. I began, searching for a new doctor, someone who could manage both the RA and now the Hep-C. Call after call I was told there was nothing that they could do; nothing would cure the RA and nothing would cure the Hep-C. I was relentless in my search and it lead me to a female physician who was willing to see me and possibly take on the challenge. After being turned down by so many I was encouraged, someone would finally see me. Now, I cannot be sure, but she might have taken me on due to the lack of clients. She was probably one of the rudest people I have ever encountered in my life, but she was willing to work with me. So, I ignored the absence of her bed-side manner, and her inability to express empathy and stayed. She ordered a battery of tests, the same tests as my previous physician. When I went in for my consult she proceeded to tell me that it was probably my fault because Hep-C can be sexually transmitted, and it was possible that I had contracted it from one of my partners.

Now, here is the part where I had to be real with myself. I was single, cute, very sexy and looking for love in all the wrong places, I can admit that. There was a time where I didn't care if the man was single, or if he was married with a wife and children. If he was interested and we made a connection, it became a relationship, of sorts. I was making up for lost time and if he could satisfy what I thought that I needed in my life, then it was a go. Could it have been my fault? At this time in my life I had been celibate for over six years. Pain had a way of neutralizing any physical desires in that area for me. It hurt for people to hug me; rolling around in the sheets with a man in my condition would not have resulted in orgasm or any type of physical pleasure I can assure you.

However, some people with Hep-C are asymptomatic and can carry the disease for years and never even know it. My case was a bit different though since I had to have my blood tested regularly because of the infusions and the drugs that I had to take for my RA; Prednisone was one of those drugs. Extended use of this drug can cause damage to the liver and sometimes diabetes, so I was always monitored closely. The fact that it had never shown up in all of these years, the elevated infection in my blood which is typically noticed in the early stages of contracting the disease and the fact that I had not been sexually active in over six years made me ask the question again, "Doc, how can it be my fault?"

After a brief pause and jotting a few notes in my chart, she began asking questions. I shared with her the episode that I had from the RA treatment and the stroke the year before. I told her about an infusion in January of 2012 that led to my being extremely ill with fever and chills that the doctor dismissed as the flu. Then I discussed with her that I had knee and back surgery in February of that same year and had difficulty in waking up from anesthesia. I ended up with an infection but was sent home from the hospital still feverish.

She was at a loss but did say maybe I had been carrying this infection for an extended amount of time. However, with the levels in my blood, the kidney failure, etc....I would have already been on dialysis, and the fact that all my prior test results had come back negative that was not the case. At this point my frustration level had escalated to the place where I would have accepted responsibility for contracting the disease if it would move someone to be willing to help me in finding a treatment.

Living away from home was wonderful for me, even with all my health challenges there was such a sense of peace that I treasured. They placed my father in Hospice care, Mom was struggling with Alzheimer's and even though I called and checked on them every day, throughout the day, I knew in my spirit that I had to return home to help. I just could not rest until I was there with them. So, I went back home for a bit. I had no Rheumatology doctor in KC anyway, so why not. My walk was a limp, and I could use my arms only minimally, but I was there with my parents doing whatever I could do to help. I was in constant pain, that was a given, but it mattered little because I was there. Within two weeks of my being there my father passed. Years before, he and Mom had already pre-planned everything. All that remained to do was the completion of a few final details for the service. We buried him on November 26th in the mausoleum he had selected.

It was time to return to KC and I determined that I was not leaving without my mother. I wanted to take care of her, I needed to take care of her. So, I moved her into my apartment with me and did my very best to surround her with love and attention. For eleven months she stayed with me, but in eleven months her disease worsened, as well as my ability to move and care for her. My health was failing fast and when I went to see the doctor they said that it was too much for me to handle. My heart broke as I accepted the realities of the situation, I had to send Momma back. I do not remember ever crying as much as I did when she left, but I knew it was for the best—for the both of us. It took only a few months for the void to widen enough for me to make changes to fill it. I moved back home in September, found an apartment close to where she lived and did as much as I could to help. I found a great family physician who referred me to a liver specialist who unbeknownst to me would change my life.

Daddy

When it comes to father's I was blessed with one of the best. Daddy was a man's man. Tall, handsome, strong. He had played football in college and spent a brief time in the military. He was old school when it came to the designation of duties around the home. His duties included working, keeping up the maintenance on the yard, the house and the cars. He would not allow my mother to wash her car, or even put gas in it, Mom's job was inside the house; the cleaning, the kids and the cooking. Now it was not that he couldn't cook because he could, and he did so on rare occasions. He could be so stubborn that he would rather starve before ever fixing a meal; not part of the division of duties. He and my mother had rules in their marriage. One of those rules was that they would never leave each other without a kiss goodbye. I am not sure when this rule was established, but I imagine it was discussed soon after they said, "I do". I remember one morning they had an argument and he stormed through the house, passed me sitting at the kitchen table, out the garage door and got in his truck. He started it up and as the garage door closed you could hear the tires as he sped out the drive heading to work. Mom had made her way to the kitchen and was doing something over at the sink. I heard the garage door raise and figured that it was one of my brothers outside fiddling around before school. When the door opened it was Daddy. He didn't say a single word, he just walked over to the sink where Mom was standing, leaned in and kissed my mother. Then he turned and marched back out the door.

Daddy was one of the first black firefighters working in our city. I remember hearing the sirens blaring and seeing the big red fire truck speeding down the street and if he was driving he always blew the horn so that we knew it was him. When he retired from the city fire department he worked as a fireman for a major aircraft manufacturer. He was a provider and made sure that we had everything we needed, a comfortable home, food on the table and most of the things that we wanted. He was a practical man who led a simple life, including being a trustee at our church. Daddy was also a HAM operator and the den at our house was his base. Trying to watch T.V. while ignoring him as he keyed the mike, "breaker, breaker this is Cougar" was nearly impossible, but we managed.

No matter what we, his children did he never judged us he just loved us through it. Now don't get me wrong, he would tell you what he thought and sometimes it hurt as the truth sometimes does. But then he would sit and determine what the next course of action needed to be. Through it all we always knew he was there for us and we put him through plenty of challenges over the years. Thinking about it now, he knew that peace that I was talking about earlier and he knew it well.

You can imagine how difficult it was for all of us when his health began to fail. At first it was numbness in his feet. The doctor's diagnosed him with diabetes, so his diet changed, and all was well. Then a tiny tack in the sole of his shoe resulted in him losing part of his foot. His foot healed, he bought new shoes, and all was well. Then he became so tired. We figured it was from the diabetes, but the doctor's said he had Leukemia and a blocked artery. He had surgery, took medication and as always, he was up and at it again.

I always felt that my father didn't deserve the health problems that he endured, not him. He was such a good, kind and wonderful man. He chose a career that required he put his life on the line for strangers and he would do anything he could to help others. No, he didn't deserve this, not him. But, he never complained he just got up and kept going, a bit slower and cautious than before but he kept going.

On November 15, 2011 the Lord called to Daddy to come home. It was one of the hardest days of my life, but I knew that he would no longer be in pain and he was no longer suffering. Peace was present as I watched him release his last breath. His spirit was free, and he left for home one final time. Breaker, breaker 1-9, Cougar is 10-7 and we gone!

XIII

Sliding Turns to Rolling to the Bottom

Sometimes going back is exactly what is needed to go forward. I met with the specialist that my family physician had referred. I was a bit apprehensive and admittedly my expectation was that the experience would not be much different than before, but I was willing and hopeful. After the specialist reviewed my charts, read my history, and ran a battery of tests. Afterward he suggested that I would be a great candidate for a new trial for the treatment and cure of Hep-C. That is all I needed to hear, cure—I was in!

As always, the Lord had answered my prayer and I was selected for the trial study of a new chemotherapy drug treatment that was proven to cure Hep C. The treatment came with a warning, it was going to take three months of shots and medication, daily. I would not be able to be around anyone, no one could touch the medication and I would need to have home health care and a visiting nurse as I went through the treatment. It was going to be very hard on my body and very painful. They could not give me much for the pain because it would interfere with the chemo, but my doctor assured me that I could do it. As I left his office I was still trying to process everything this treatment would entail. If I did this it would be three months of chemo injections, seven days a week.

I would be isolated to my one-bedroom apartment for the entire time. Then there were the costs of the treatment; $10,000 per injection. Medicare wasn't going to foot the bill and I didn't have those kinds of resources. No, this was too much, way too much- I'm out! When I got home I called and shared my concerns with my doctor, thanked him and began to prepare my heart to live life with this disease.

Now faith is the substance of things hoped for, and I was hoping and praying for healing. I petitioned the Lord and simply asked Him to work things out if this was HIS plan for me to get this treatment. Unbeknownst to me, the specialist had written letters to the board of directors conducting the study. He told me that it took two denials before they agreed to allow me into the program, and-----all costs would be covered. I was flooded with both joy and angst all at once. How was I going to get through all of this alone? This was dangerous, and I was at risk of losing my life, was I ready to take this on? Was going to have to give myself the shots, was I going to be able to do it? Enough! Here was the help that I had asked for, here was my answered prayer. I was scared, but one thing that I knew for sure, God had never left me, and HE wouldn't leave me now. I'm all in—again.

My treatment began. I have to say that it was worse than anything that I could have possibly imagined or put into words. First, I had to live pretty much in isolation. The medication was very dangerous, too dangerous for anyone other than a trained professional, my nurse to handle. After the first round of injections I was allowed some family and friends to come and visit, but they had to be gloved and masked. They couldn't touch me or any of the meds, it was dangerous for them to come in contact with this stuff. It could have resulted in their becoming ill from exposure to it, so I made sure that visits were brief, and all of the rules were followed.

I was confident that in the end this was all going to be worth it but trying to see how I was going to make it to end was really beginning to become blurry for me. Let me walk you through what my life looked like every day. I vomited every day. I lost so much weight that I was nothing more than skin and bones. I looked like a skeleton. Even though I now weighed less than 100 pounds, most of the time I was too weak to walk so I crawled to the toilet. One morning I awoke, got out of the bed and felt light headed, not the normal light headedness; I was light of hair. My head looked like plugs had been pulled from it, so I grabbed some scissors and cut all of it off. When taking my injections, no one could come near me. They could not be in my room when I was taking it, especially anyone who was pregnant or wanted to eventually conceive children, woman or man.

This stuff I was taking was strong and it was dangerous; Interferon, Ribavirin and Sovaldi-all at once along with four additional drugs. These were the main characters in the play, along with other supporting actors. I played my part and took my injections religiously; this play was real, organic and used no makeup and no props. I began to look so bad that I was afraid for my grandchildren to see me for fear that I would become the monster they see in bad dreams.

I spent my days lying in bed or sitting on the couch. Sometimes I would watch church services on the television, or online. I would read my Bible and hold onto Isiah 53:5, NKJV "by His stripes we are healed." I read that scripture over and over. When I took my treatments, I repeated it; when I went to bed, I repeated it; when I woke up I repeated it. I prayed and prayed that this was all going to be worth it in the end, I held on to my faith and belief that I was healed.

My Sister would come to visit, even with her hands full raising her family and taking care of our mother, she was always such an encouragement and support. At times my suffering made her angry and caused her to question why they had not put me in the hospital to do this. She couldn't understand how could they allow a person go through this without constant help there? My friend-cousin, that name you give someone who doesn't share blood but is family nonetheless, was a God-send bringing me ready-made meals and tons of water. She lives a life of helping others, it is her gift. I am a grateful recipient of that help and love. Another cousin would come through and sit with me, pray with me and bring me whatever it was that I might need. She kept a loving, watchful eye over me. I talked with my sister in Florida all the time, usually at night when the pain was great she would stay on the phone with me. One of those nights I was telling her that one of the side effects of the treatment was flu like symptoms and that I was freezing all of the time. No matter what, I just could not stay warm. Before our conversation ended, she told me that my electric blanket was on the way.

As difficult as the treatment was on me, it was equally so for my children. My daughter still lived in KC, working and raising her children, but she called daily, several times daily. It hurt her heart not being there, and it hurt mine too. Each time she called to let me know that she was coming to see me I got so excited! She would come in gloved and gowned and would commence to cleaning, cooking and caring for all of my needs. My daughter was my rock and my support all of the way.

As for my son, things were a bit different, or so I thought. At the start of my treatment, he would come over and stock my cabinets and refrigerator full of food; soups, crackers, cheese and fruit. He would fidget around a bit and then leave. Soon after, his visits became less frequent, but he called every day. Initially I was hurt that he didn't come by more often since he lived right around the corner, and then I realized why. He is a man and by nature, designed to protect. I had not paid attention to the hurt in his eyes as he saw me crawl to the bathroom. I missed the tears in his eyes as he watched me writhe in pain. I didn't hear his heart weep each time he heard me moan. I finally realized that his feelings of helplessness because he knew that there was nothing that he could do to protect me from this situation were at the base of the absence of his physical presence. Once I came to this understanding, my hurt left. My son loves me and just hearing his voice over the phone provided me such joy and comfort.

Sometimes people start a journey with you and then fall away as time goes on, but not my family and not my friends. Every week my aunts called me from Chicago, my dad's sisters, both of them were up in age, 80 and 90 years old, but they took the time to check on me. My sisters would call and pray with me, encourage me to press on. My cousin blessed me with a bed side toilet, so I wouldn't have to crawl to the bathroom. It was amazing how God knew what I needed when I needed it. I remember one day my cousin called to say she would be by in about fifteen minutes. I had given her a key to the apartment so that she could come in and out because it took so long for me to get to the door. When she came in, she found me passed out on the floor and was able to get some assistance right away. The Lord knows what you need and when you need it, and one thing is certain, I would not have made it without them all, each and every one of them.

Six weeks in, I had to go to the doctor for a blood draw, so they could check my numbers. As he picked up the file to review the lab results, he looked at me, trying to be encouraging he said, "Let's see how well you are progressing." As he read and flipped the pages back and forth, his brow began to furrow. I couldn't read his expression, was this concern that the treatment wasn't working? Maybe it was working but not as quickly as he had hoped? I sat there waiting, and I will admit it, I was a bit anxious. When finally, he spoke, I could hear him, but I was not sure that his words were registering—for either of us. There was nothing there, there were no numbers to review because the disease was no longer there. He shared that they had never seen anything like this, lower numbers yes, but nothing at all, never.

The words started way down deep in my belly, moved up through my chest and made their way into my throat, "Thank you, Lord, thank YOU LORD!" In my thinking, no numbers, no trace of the disease meant no more treatments were necessary, but I was wrong, I had to complete the series which meant another six weeks of darkness. I left the office weak, sick, tired and totally elated. There is a God in heaven who loves me, "thank you Jesus".

I had become so weak that they had approved a home health aide to come and assist me with things around the house and I was thankful. During this same time the agency changed my nurse. After one week I realized that the nurse that they had assigned me was unprepared to manage my case. She didn't take things seriously and spent too much time playing around. For this treatment to be effective you cannot miss an injection, not one. She was less than attentive one week and pulled out the needle before pushing all of the meds and I ended up with them all over my shirt instead of in my arm. Wow, $10,000 down the drain and worse, I didn't get all of my medications. Needless to say, I had to report the incident to her agency and replaced her that same day. I was so afraid that this interruption was going to set me back, but fortunately it didn't. I was able to continue and was assigned one of the most comical, supportive and caring nurses in the world.

The remaining weeks continued the same as the first six with all of the symptoms still presenting themselves. I suppose I was expecting that they would subside because from all reports from the tests there was nothing there but that was not the case. When I completed my final injection, I had to wait for a month before going in to have my blood work done again. I also had to have a complete physical work up to ensure that everything was functioning properly. I was excited, and I felt victorious, I had beat cancer twice and now add to my belt Hep-C, oh, I was on cloud nine.

If it were possible for me to skip on my way into the office of my specialist I certainly would have, but instead I settled for a lilt in my wobbled step which was more than enough for me. It was impossible for me to stop smiling as I listened to my results, there were no traces of the disease in my blood, my liver, or my body. There were tears and hugs and thank you all-around, I was cured, thank you Jesus, I was cured. By this time my daughter and her family had moved to Texas and once she heard that I was cured, she made a declaration that I was moving to Texas with her so that she could make sure that I was cared for.

She made it a point to do exactly that, get me moved. I had to have both a liver specialist and a general practitioner to follow up my care and to make sure that everything continued to improve. I am not sure how she accomplished such a feat; however, she was able to schedule both appointments for the same day. I saw the liver specialist that morning around 10 am and everything went great. The next stop was my general practitioner for my physical exam, a necessary formality when ending this type of horrendous treatment. They took me back and checked my blood pressure, temperature and weighed me, all was good with the exception of my weight which was very low. I had dropped down to under a hundred pounds by this point, but I didn't really care. I was sure that my appetite would return in short order.

The medical assistant escorted me to an exam room and I disrobed and put on a gown, and sat on the exam table waiting for the doctor to come in. When she did come in, she was smiling and as pleasant as usual and even more so once I shared the positive results of the treatment.

We talked as she checked my ears, nose and throat. She listened to my goings on at the same time as she had me to inhale and exhale deeply. We talked while she examined one breast and we talked while she examined the other, and then she stopped talking. She pushed and moved my breast under her hands, she stopped and repeated the movements again. I had also stopped talking and instead I was looking intently into her face, holding my breath as she looked at me and said, "You have lumps in your breast".

She made a call and an immediate appointment for me to see a breast surgeon that day, who completed an additional set of exams, x-rays and tests. I consider this favor because it is unheard of to get through the process as quickly as I did that day. I remember very clearly the fear that rose inside of me when the radiologist came in after reading my films. He took my hand in his and said that he realized that I had already been through so much, but that I needed to have a biopsy and he wanted to have it done that same day.

At that moment I could not wrap my head around what was going on, so I told him no, there was no way that I could endure anything more in this day. My emotions had gone from elation to feeling like someone was inside my body with a serrated edged knife cutting pieces from my heart. How was I going to tell my children this, and even more, how was I going to endure it?

XIV

Crumpled at the Bottom of the Hill

It took no time for the results to return, and for my world to once again spin out of control. The lumps were cancerous, they were malignant, and they were aggressive; I was diagnosed with Triple Negative breast cancer. The suggested recourse was to undergo a Mastectomy and remove the entire breast and it had to be done so without hesitation, followed by several rounds of chemotherapy. I saw her lips moving, I heard what she was saying, but it just would not register. I could not process it. As she was speaking, all that was repeating in my mind was a sermon by Bishop T.D Jakes that I had heard sometime earlier, 'This Is Not The Time To Lose Your Head'. Sermon on YouTube 2017. I had completed my Hep-C treatment at the end of September, had received my all clear at the end of October; it was early November and now this; I couldn't even cry.

I made the decision to undergo a modified radical Mastectomy on both breasts having all of the breast tissue, and lymph nodes removed. Triple Negative breast cancer can be more difficult to treat, is more likely to spread and to recur. Even though the other breast seemed to be healthy I wanted to reduce the chance of this recurring in my future so both had to go. They took me through genetic testing, to see if I had inherited the BRCA1 gene mutation. I thank God that I didn't carry the gene. I was able to breathe a bit easier knowing that my daughter and granddaughter would not inherit this from me. The advice from the surgeon was that this needed to happen quickly, so I prepared my mind and my heart. I was ready, let's do this. Then came the no, my surgery had to be delayed. The holiday season interfered with the surgery schedule, so I had to wait until the 2nd week of December. I enjoyed Thanksgiving with my family and for a brief moment I was able to dismiss thoughts of my impending surgery. During the couple of weeks, as I waited for my surgery I must have given the news and repeated the story fifty times to family and friends. I think most had a similar reaction of disbelief as I did when the doctor first told me.

Allow me to help you understand just how aggressive this cancer was. I have a small frame and typically never carried much weight. My breasts were a beautiful D cup and they were very dense and sometimes heavy. After having my lumpectomy, I was required to have a mammogram every 3 months, then every 6 months and about three years prior to this diagnosis it was required once per year. I had actually had my annual mammogram at the beginning of the year prior to my Hep-C treatment. I never noticed anything different about my breasts, however with everything going on with my treatment I was distracted. When my general practitioner examined me there were seven lumps in my breast. Three weeks later and three days before my surgery my oncologist found three more lumps had grown. If I can offer any advice to women it is simply this, check yourself on a regular basis. Regardless of what might be going on in your life, take a few minutes at least once per month to do a self-examination of your breasts. If you feel something, or you see something that is not normal for you, see your doctor right away.

The night before my surgery I could not seem to settle myself down. I was packing this, searching for that, writing something in one journal then transferring it to another; just keeping myself busy. It was about eleven o'clock at night and I was still at it, when there was a knock on the door. My daughter went down and opened it and of course I was asking who was there. She said nothing so of course I started to get up, and as I did I saw my sister from Florida ascending the stairs. I screamed and literally jumped and wrapped my arms around her neck for a while. When I finally released her from my grasp, I looked at her and told her that I couldn't believe that she was here. Her reply, "you didn't think I was going to let you go through this without me here, did you?". Now I was ready, I had my angels watching over me, soldiers by my side; my daughter, my sister and my cousins, it was time to get in the fight.

We arrived at the hospital and they took me back immediately. They got me prepped and ready for surgery. Just before going into the operating room my surgeon came to my bedside and asked if we could pray. My heart leaped, and I said of course, but asked if I could have my family come back and join us, he agreed. Before I knew it, the entire area was filled with people, my daughter, my sister, my cousins, a couple of my adopted daughters; nurses and doctors in scrubs, even a lady who had been cleaning stopped to join in. In that moment I was surrounded by angels on all sides, some that I could see and others that I could not, but I knew they were there because I could feel them. "Are they not all ministering spirits sent out to serve those who are going to inherit salvation?" (Hebrews 1:14, CSB).

XV

Up the Next Hill

The surgery was a success. It took a bit longer than expected but my doctor was pleased and confident that they had gotten everything. By early afternoon I was moved to my hospital room, hooked to the monitors and my recovery began. I was bandaged tightly around my chest and I had drainage tubes on both sides of my body. I was on morpheein for the pain, so I was comfortable. Just as it had been before surgery, so it was now in my room, I was surrounded by people who loved me. I was winning!

The second day after surgery the nurse came in to tell me that I was going to need a port put in so that they could administer the chemotherapy. They had already examined me and had decided that the best placement for the port would be my chest. Lord, help me, please not more surgery, but it had to be done so I agreed. They discharged me after two days in the hospital and I went home. My sister was able to stay with me for two-weeks, but then had to return back to her home and work. My daughter, cousins and grandchildren kept a vigilant watch over me and made sure that I was following all of the doctor's instructions.

It finally came time for me to go in for my checkup. The breast surgeon was happy with how my healing was progressing. I guess it was part of procedure, but when she exited the room another surgeon entered and began to discuss my breast reconstruction surgery. I interrupted him and asked him who it was that said that I was interested in reconstruction. He stated that he was there to do a consult and answer my questions. According to him most women elect to have this surgery, so he was just getting it out of the way, so he could get me on his schedule.

In listening to him talk it became apparent that he believed that somehow a woman did not feel complete without having breasts. Wrong! I had a beautiful pair of breasts, but they tried to kill me. They were gone now, and I had no plans on replacing them with implants. Now, please understand, I am not saying that women should not have breast reconstruction if that is what they choose. What I am saying is that not having breast reconstruction was the right choice for me. I was insulted by his assumptions and I told him as much. I wish I had taken a picture of how far his jaw dropped when I told him that I wasn't interested, and a video of his slamming his notebook shut and stomping out of the exam room. He was not happy with me to say the least and I didn't care.

My next stop was to meet with my Oncologist to discuss my chemotherapy treatment plan. He took his time in explaining to me how this procedure would work. I would have to come to the hospital and be hooked up via the port in my chest to a machine that would administer the medication. He then began to discuss the several types of chemotherapy drugs that would be used in my treatment, one of which had been nicknamed red devil because of how strong it was. Imagine his surprise when I told him that I would not take the drug until they began to refer to it as something else; I was not allowing anything with that name in my body. Cancer had already tried to take me out, there was no way I was going to accept the devil in any part of my treatment, even if it was just a nickname.

I began my treatment, and week after week I would lay on the table while gowned, masked and gloved nurses picked and prodded at me and then hooked me up to the machines. As I lay there watching them come in and out I would sometimes feel like I was some monster that people were afraid of being near in fear that I would infect them. This of course was the furthest thing from the truth, in actuality they were doing this for my protection. My immune system was so compromised that an infection could be very dangerous for me. Once satisfied that everything had checked out they would start the machine and the medicine would enter my body. I would immediately feel a burning sensation as it moved through my veins, my entire body felt like it was on fire from the inside; every nerve, every muscle, every bone and cell were set ablaze by these drugs, it was awful. Then came the nausea, the vomiting, and the chills. I would lay on the bed, sometimes feeling like it was my deathbed, and staring upward praying, Lord God, please get me through this.

At one point I felt like I was going to die which was at the point where I was probably going to. It had been less than six months between completing my Hep-C treatments which were of course a form of chemotherapy and beginning this round of chemotherapy for my breast cancer. It had been almost two years in total having these extremely strong drugs in my system and it was killing me, literally. A bucket can only hold so much, and my body had reached the limit; they had to back me off of the stronger drugs and create a different treatment plan to finish out the regimen.

This made the doctors uncomfortable because they were not sure that all of the cancer cells could be destroyed with lessening the drugs, however there were no other options. I received it as an answered prayer, my time of this type of suffering was ending, the Lord had said enough.

XVI

Nearing the top of the Hill

My chemotherapy treatments had ended, it was now time for my body to begin the healing process; it was now time for my body to begin to regenerate. I wish at this point in my story I could tell you that the regeneration process was smooth and uneventful, but I cannot. I had repeated visits to the emergency room because of various reactions to the drugs as they were processing out of my body. I would double over in excruciating pain and have to be taken in to be seen and given pain medication to manage. I had rashes that would appear out of now where making my skin raw in places. My throat would become so swollen and sore that I could barely eat, drink or speak. Then my heart started giving me problems, so they put me on medication to control my blood pressure. It took some time for them to finally get it regulated from the drastic fluctuations high to low, but it is now manageable. My RA symptoms had pretty much gone away with the chemo; however, they came back with a vengeance once the drugs were no longer holding it at bay.

Then there was my hair. I had lost a lot of my hair during my Hep-C treatments, but it had grown back. During the chemotherapy for my breast cancer it had begun to come out in large plugs, so much so that I opted to shave it all off. I sported my bald head proudly, very rarely covering it up. People would see me out and about and would come and share their stories with me. The loss of a mother, a sister, or a wife became frequent conversations between me and perfect strangers.

An interesting thing happened each time I had these types of encounters. I found that most of the persons who engaged in a conversation with me about my fight with cancer found a sense of peace being able to share their experience with me. What always began as them offering me encouragement usually ended with them telling me thank you. Who knew that my bald head would be a ministry tool?

It was also my bald head that allowed me to meet some wonderful ladies who had survived just like I had. I might be walking down the street or through the store or sitting at a table in a restaurant and see a woman with a bald head like mine. Our eyes would lock, and we would nod, smile and make our way over to greet one another. Sometimes it was just that one encounter, other times it resulted in an exchange of telephone numbers. There was no official group, just random ladies willing to pick up the phone and call and check on each other since none of us knew what each day would hold. It was a bit like being a sponsor for AA, you just had to be prepared to deal with what might be shared on the other end of the line.

I will never forget one young lady who after being clear for two years called me to say that her cancer had recurred. She was devasted and we prayed together for a while. A few weeks passed, and I called to check on her but was unable to get hold of her. A few more weeks passed, and I tried again, still nothing.

On my third attempt a few weeks later a young man answered the phone. I told him who I was, and his voice brightened. He recognized my name and said that his mother talked about me all the time. The conversation continued for a minute or two more and then he told me that she had gone home to be with the Lord. My heart sank, and tears welled in my eyes. I held it together long enough to get through the rest of the call but when I hung up the phone, I cried. Like it or not, this is the reality of surviving cancer, you just never know if it will rear its ugly head again in your life.

I thank God daily for my healing and I move with no fear that I will have to engage in fighting with cancer ever again. My hair grew back, but not like it once was; it will not grow longer than about an inch. Sure, there are other challenges that remain, but I truly believe that cancer will not be one that I have to deal with ever again.

XVII

Back on Top of the Hill

It has been three years since my victory over cancer. I have learned and grown so much in this amount of time it amazes me. If someone had ever told me that I would be strong enough to endure the entirety of this situation I would have called them a liar. There is no way possible that I could have done this on my own, no, it was the love of God and my trust in HIM that gave me my strength. I wanted to give up so many times, but then I would look at my grandchildren and realize that I wanted to live, and I had to fight.

The word of God is described as a two-edged sword and I wielded it as such; it accomplished everything that it was sent out to do. It brought me peace, strength, direction, and provided me with the power to stand. I never stood alone because I was surrounded by love, angels, family and friends. It brought me healing, and not only my body, but my mind and my spirit were healed as well.

When I look back over my life, HIS grace and protection is evident. My mind was made up on what I wanted to do. All of the wrong choices created plenty of damage and hurt to go around for anyone near me, but more so for myself. When I made my choice to turn back to HIM, everything changed, and it changed for the better. For some, this might seem confusing, that I would say things changed for the better because of the health issues that kept showing up, so let me explain.

The feelings of regret and guilt over the many wrong choices that I had made in my life were gone. No longer was I reaching into my closet of skeletons, or allowing someone else to do so, and grabbing a bone and beating myself up with it; I was free. I had owned up to all my mess and returned it all to the cross where Jesus had nailed it all. I asked for forgiveness and I have been forgiven. I repented and turned away from my past and turned my focus on what the Lord had next for me.

My next came in the form of a fight, well, several fights for my life, and with each victory I became stronger in my walk with the Lord. I learned that I must hold on to Gods hands--always. You see, choosing to follow Christ does not make you exempt from trouble, but it does give you the protection and ability to overcome it.

As an added benefit, you get to become someone new. I am a new person in Christ Jesus, with a new mind and a renewed spirit, look at me, I just wrote my first book! Every day I wake up and HE has placed something on my heart to share, so now I send an encouraging message to family and friends daily. All of this is so far past my comfort zone and certainly nothing that I would or could have imagined that I would be doing, but I am, and I give all honor and glory to the Lord above for it all.

The truth is this, no matter what you do or don't do, the storms of life will keep coming. Ask yourself, these two questions, one, would you rather face them down alone, or would you rather face them with the creator of heaven and earth? Two, would you prefer to face the unknown alone, or with the one who knows the number of hairs on your head? Only you can answer those questions for yourself, but as for me I chose the God that knows my past and loved me anyway. The God who covered my sins under the blood and doesn't see them anymore. The God who sacrificed his only son for me, Jesus Christ, my Savior, so that I can live forever. I have no idea of what life experiences are ahead of me, but this I do know, I will never have to face them alone.

XVIII

Winding Roads

The dips and hills are now much easier to climb, maybe because they have become familiar. I cannot tell you that it is all over at this point, no, the challenges continue in the maneuvering through the damage done to my body from all the chemotherapy that was used in treating me. Along with my preexisting Rheumatoid Arthritis, a new issue that has developed with my blood pressure.

My bones have become brittle now because the marrow has been destroyed and it takes time for the red blood cells to regenerate themselves. I must be careful so that I don't bump around too much at this point, a lesson I learned the hard way. A simple stubbing of my toe resulted in a small fracture that put me into a boot for weeks, and even now still has not healed completely. My RA has returned with a vengeance and I wrestle back and forth with it but changing my diet and using herbal supplements helps.

The most challenging issue right now is that my blood pressure fluctuates from extreme highs to extreme lows repeatedly throughout the day and night. I have had numerous medications in varying doses and the problem remains. Additional testing indicates that one of the valves in my heart is not functioning as it should because of the chemotherapy, but surgery is out of the question in my case. I know that at some point my heart and blood pressure will come into alignment, until then I will accept that it is due to the fullness of the love that continues to fill my heart.

If all of that is not enough I have had a bout with Bronchitis after having been hospitalized for vertigo and a cyst, of which everything has been attributed in some way to my having had chemotherapy.

Oh, and there is one more thing, my hair. Prior to this journey my head was covered with thick, full, long brown strands of hair. It began to come out, no matter how I tried to condition and keep it, it just could not hold on. It has grown back now, but just enough for me to wear it in a tiny, curly close cut 'fro; it won't grow longer than that. I have become comfortable with my new look and like I said before, it has become part of my ministry, my crowning glory!

There are bad days and there are good days, but more and more the good days are starting to outnumber the bad ones and for me that is encouraging. It may not sound too encouraging many of you, but for me it means that my prayers are being answered and I am progressing forward in total healing and restoration of my body.

~

It is in you Lord Jesus that I live and move and breath and have my being, use me Lord. AMEN

My Daily Thought Sharing

On a daily basis, I find joy and fulfillment in sharing what God puts on my heart as an encouragement to myself and others. I would often add graphical features to these words of inspiration and share with family and friends. I hope these might inspire you as well.

Joy Center!

Directions in the night, waking up before the daylight. Who can you call on? HE is still up, 24 hours, 7 days a week. HE will hear you calling HIS name. Keep Jesus the center of your life, everything will work out. Trust him. Your faith will bring you through. Remember HE is there 24 hours, no one is like him. Glorify HIS name.

Which Way to Go?

Waking up this morning your Spirit filling with praise, are you listening to the Lord? Inside your Spirit hearing his love in your heart. Time to get started for the day. Your steps have been ordered. Let God handle your steps today, it is already done!

Examine Your Heart!

Have you ever taken the time to see what is inside of your heart? Have you ever listened to the voice that's call you to let him inside of your heart? If we spell heart on a piece of paper, you find in the word (hear) the word of God in your heart. (Ear), God gave us ears to hear, and (art) the art of God's love written in HIS book. Examine our heart, God has a plan for you.

Don't Worry

Ruler, tape measure, calculators; looking for something to count with and to measure. Counting numbers so high, as high as they go, but there is no need to count or to measure, God will not give you more than you can handle! When you go through, count it all joy because God will bring you through!

Printed in the United States
By Bookmasters